IBM PRISON POET

&

A FABLE:

MADOFF MOVE OVER !

BY

MADAME P. J. BAILEY

ISBN-10:0615551017

ISBN-13:978-0615551012 (MADAME P J BAILEY PUBLICATIONS)

DEDICATION

TO ALL PERSONS IN POSITIONS OF AUTHORITY.

*"For what shall it profit a man, if he shall gain the whole world, and lose his own soul ?
Or what shall a man give in exchange for his soul ?"*

Mark 8:36,37

CONTENTS

PREFACE

Writing and wcb site development became my frustration relief valves as I feuded with high powered lawyers during my 10 year slugfest with IBM ! This volume of poetry is the result of some of my outpourings. "If The Gray Hat Fits" was my initial vent. There was a long break before I penned "IBM's Ball Game". I hit my stride when IBM heir apparent, Sr. VP Robert "Blabber Mouth" Moffat, was arrested, confessed, and did time in prison. Insult was added to injury with the commencement of the IBM PONZI RICO litigation. What an eye opener !!!

Many of the poems are based on Sing-a-long tunes. The links to those tunes are posted on http://ibmTheWidowMaker.com

IBM: The Widow Maker is my memorial tribute to my late husband, Philip J. Bailey, Jr. (See http://ibmTheWidowMaker.com for background information.) Philip devoted over 25 years to IBM. His life was cut short at age 56 due to multiple myeloma. That cancer leaves a human skeleton looking like Swiss cheese. IBM needlessly exposed Philip and thousands of other trusting workers to harsh industrial strength chemicals during their employment. As a result, many IBM employees and their off-springs suffered painful, disfiguring illnesses and deaths. Many received no compensation. Others were offered insulting take-it-or-leave-it pittances. Many more individuals world-wide are walking time bombs. IBM has yet to take a proactive stance to encourage exposed former and current employees to seek testing to determine whether they have been affected by their work place exposure.

I have undertaken to sound the Warning Call both far and wide through the "IBM Widow's Wish List Campaign". 10% of the net sale proceeds of this and related works will fund this public awareness effort.

Moffat's Post-Prison Advisory

I once wore a kilt,

Kept stiff upper lip.

When cuffed, didn't flip,

Stuck to lawyer's script.

Did 6 month jail "dip",

Now offer this tip:

When tempted to slip,

Don't kiss or unzip !

Ode To "Blabber Mouth" Moffat

There once was an Exec named Moffat,

Who succeeded in lining his pocket

At IBM, SMART PLANET,

He angled, finagled,

'Til he reached the Number 2 Socket !

But Moffat, Poor Chum, had loose lips,

A penchant for a blonde with loose hips.

He talked and he dropped

The few words that she sought,

And now he will pay,

'Cause he's caught !

Little Ms. Tough-It

Little Ms. Tough-It,

Sat on a Moffat,

Scheming and weaving her tale.

She sat down beside him,

Then smiled, turned the lights dim,

Now Moffat is facing the jail !

Somebody's Knocking

Sing-a-long Tune: "Somebody's Knocking At Your Door"

Somebody's knocking at your door, your door. [2X]
Big Blue Insider, why don't you answer ?
Somebody's knocking at your door.

Could it be the SEC this time, this time ? [2X]
Big Blue Insiders, 2-late-2-run-4-cover.
Could it be the SEC this time ?

'Fess up, save your clever tales for jail, for jail. [2X]
Big Blue Insiders, why don't you answer ?
'Fess up, save your clever tales for jail.

You have done the crime, now do the time, the time. [2X]
Big Blue Insiders, you SMART PLANETeerers.
You have done the crime, now do the time.

O-Bandits, O-Bandits
(An Ode To Inside Traders)

Sing-a-long Tune: "The Holy City"

One night as I lay scheming,
There came a dream, a dare:
I'll sell my stock, skim off the top,
Leave others unaware.
My cut buddies signed on with me,
We plotted day and night.

And when I signaled, they cashed in,
And squealed with such delight. [2X]

Chorus –

O-Bandits, O-Bandits, lift up your voices, sing.
O-Bandits, IBM's brightest,
March on, let our faces beam.

We got over, year after year,
We thought we were so SMART !
We've beat the rest, 'cause we're The Best.
Plus, we've got so much charm.
Surely no one will ever guess,
Our plans are good as gold.

We'll rob the bank, until it tanks,
Grab riches yet untold. [2X]

Chorus –

O-Bandits, O-Bandits,
Toast to our stealth and wealth.
O-Bandits, the SMARTest PLANET,
What lucky hands we've been dealt !!!

And then, at once, my dream switched up,
New visions came to me:
I saw the ugly finish, besides The Tax Man's feet.
The SEC swooped down on me, the FBI pursued.
My lawyers start to sweat big drops:
"They've caught onto my ruse !"
It's too late to cover my tracks,
No time to change my game.

I'll have to put on my game face,
And bluff as best I can. [2X]

Chorus –

O-Bandits, O-Bandits, Let now our voices wail.
O-Bandits, we're caught red-handed,
'Fess up, let our remorse begin !!!
O-Bandits, we're caught red-handed,
'Fess up, let our remorse begin !!!

Look On The SUNny Side

Big Blue came to take them away ? Ho ! Ho !

Was that the intent from the door ? So ! So !

Big Blue went to peep, 'cause Sun Micro's unique;

They duped, got the scoop, then let out a whoop.

They pulled a fast one, then ran from The Sun.

Big Blue hit the floor with a run. Hey ! Wo !

Does Your Big Blue Stock Lose Value ?
(chorus only)

Does your Big Blue stock lose value on your bed post over night?

If the CEO, Big Execs sell theirs quickly, that's a slight !

And they make out like some bandits, stiff investors, left and right !

Does your Big Blue stock lose value on your bed post over night ?

The More We Look At Stock Trades

The more we look at stock trades,
At stock trades, at stock trades.
The more we look at stock trades,
The less happy we'll be.
'Cause Big Sam fleeced Big Blue. [2X]
The more we look at stock trades,
The less happy we'll be.

The more we question Big Sam,
Ask Big Sam 'bout his stocks.
The more we question Big Sam,
The less happy we'll be.
'Cause Big Sam is clever, a fleet-footed fella.
The more we question Big Sam,
The less happy we'll be.

The more we quiz Big Execs
At big Blue, at Big Blue;
The more we quiz Big Execs,
Their stories unglue.
'Cause he said that you said,
That I said, that she said.
The more we quiz Big Execs,
Their stories unglue.

Let them all serve time together,
Together, together.
Let them all serve time together,
Join Madoff and pals !
'Cause SMART PLANETeerers
Think they are superior.
Let them all serve time together,
Join Madoff and pals !

IBM'S BALL GAME

Big Sam has rigged the ball game.

Big Sam has tricked the crowds.

Big Sam cashed options and stock awards;

Big Sam couldn't care if the Dow Jones does fall !

Big Sam routes, routes, routes for retirement,

"A market crash ? What a shame ?"

Public - 1, 2, 3 strikes, you Chumps,

At Big Sam's ball game !

A – B – C – D'S

A – B – C – D,   don't play dumb.

E – F – G – H, I don't believe you Chums !

J – K – L, Me not pleased.

N – O – P, It was no breeze.

Q – R – S – T, This won't work -

U mistook me for some jerk !

Z – Y – W – V, U surely know,

Trouble's waiting at your door.

S – R – Que from your lawyer(s).

P – O – N, Clean your desk drawer !

M – L – K, Justice prevails.

Gee, so sorry, you're in jail !!!

Does Your Head Hang Low ?

Does your head hang low

As you enter prison's door ?

Does your memory dwell,

Focus on what is in store ?

Does your family's faces

Grow strained, drained, pained,

More and more ?

Does your head hang low ?

IBMketeers Theme Song

I love me,

You love you,

We're "Complicity Big Blue".

We're multi-millionaires, Ho ! Ho !

With some sneers from me to you !

Don't you want to gouge, Part II ?

IBM's Dough-Re-Me

DOUGH - So dear, Big Sam holds near.

Raid – The coffers of Big Blue.

Me – Me, me, me, me, and I.

Farce – That Big Sam ran on you.

Sow – Seeds fast, time not Sam's friend.

Lo - li - gag, You might pretend.

Tea – Leaves say this will not end !

And that brings us back to DOUGH, DOUGH, DOUGH, DOUGH,

DOUGH, DOUGH, DOUGH, MORE, MORE, MORE MORE

Raze – Sam's treasure: Fed's got you !

Me – "Who else deserves so much ?"

Far – "I've grown beyond Big Blue !"

So – "I'll skip off of the scene, Ha, Ha, Ha !"

Lo – "Behold, I'll fade out fast."

Tee – "You'll find me on the greens."

"Dude – Just watch me while I thumb my nose, nose, nose !"
[Repeat verse 1 & 2 Ad Nauseum.]

IBM's Song That Has No End

Big Sam's stock trades, they have no end.

Cute trades go on and on, my friend.

Big Blue Execs got stock awards, took options,

Flipped in disguised sales,

And they'll continue trading as

They're marching off to jail !

So IBM's song, it has no end,

Just sing it on and on, my friend.

SMART PLANETeerers – bright minds will design,

Will plot, and plan, and sell,

And they'll continue trading as they're marching off to jail….

[Repeat verses 1 & 2 until your throat is sore !]

We Masters Of The Universe

We Masters of the universe,

We trade stocks, we plot, we rehearse.

We're so SMART, we had no regards –

We thought that we'd just stuff our purse !

Refrain:

Oh, Oh, Feds work wonders, Feds work nights.

Fed's investigate: our plight !

Schemings, gleanings, still proceeding,

Brought us to our saddest night.

Bernie Madoff needs some cell mates.

We cast our lots, that settled our fates.

SMART PLANETeerers, soon will deliver,

Moffat to comfort Madoff !

[Repeat Refrain.]

Sing A Song Of Millions

Sing a song of millions,

A billion waits in store !

Pockets full of greenbacks,

Who could ask for more ???

But I wasn't counting

On FBI's sting !

Isn't that the very thing

To land me in Sing-Sing ?

Humpty Big Blue (Versions 1 & 2)

Version 1

Humpty Big Blue sat proud and tall.

Humpty Big Blue soon had a great fall.

POTUS, and all of his men,

Won't glue Big Blue back together again !

Version 2

Humpty Big Blue sits on a wall.

Will Humpty Big Blue have a great fall ?

When "Blabber Mouth" Moffat opens his lips,

Will DJIA then start to flip ?

1-Little, 2-Little, 3 SMART PLANETeerers

1-Little, 2-Little, 3 SMART PLANETeerers.

4-Little, 5-Little, 6 Big Blue Executives,

7-Little, 8-Little, 9 Inside Traders,

10 SEC Agents pursue !

10-Little, 9-Little, 8 Execs start drafting,

7-Little, 6-Little, 5 long "explanations".

4-Little, 3-Little, 2 high priced lawyers,

Praying: "FBI, please don't look our way !"

IBM Comes Tumbling Down

IBM comes tumbling down, tumbling down, tumbling down.

IBM comes tumbling down, so early in the century.

Did you purchase some Big Blue shares, Big Blue shares, Big Blue shares ?

Did you purchase some Big Blue shares, too early in the century ?

Would you like to turn back the clock, back the clock, back the clock ?

Would you like to turn back the clock to early in the century ?

Skip The Blame Game, your fate's the same, fate's the same, fate's the same.

Skip The Blame Game, your fate's the same, it's early in the century !

The SMART PLANET looks not so bright, not so bright, not so bright.

The SMART PLANET looks not so bright, this early in the century.

IBM comes tumbling down, tumbling down, tumbling down.

IBM comes tumbling down, so early in the century.

Buffalo, Move Over !

Home, on SMART PLANET,

Where Big Sam and his honchos doth roam.

Where seldom is heard, any unrehearsed word,

Big Blue skies are not CLOUD-y most days !

Home, home behind bars,

SMARTie's sticky fingers doth roam.

Where often is heard remorse among words,

Big Blue skies remain CLOUD-y most days.

This Big Sam

This Big Sam, he played 1,
He laughed loud and flicked his thumb,
He said: "Sit back on a tack, throw these chumps a bone !"
This Big Sam went rolling on.

This Big Sam, he played 2,
Displayed no fear, took off his shoe,
He said: "Sit back on a tack, throw these chumps a bone !"
This Big Sam went rolling on.

This Big Sam, he played 3,
He'll bring the Dow Jones to its knee.
He said: "Sit back on a tack, throw these chumps a bone !"
This Big Sam went rolling on.

This Big Sam, he played 4,
Question him, you'll see the door.
He said: "Sit back on a tack, throw these chumps a bone !"
This Big Sam went rolling on.

This Big Sam, he played 5,
He took investors for a ride,
He said: "Sit back on a tack, throw these chumps a bone !"
This Big Sam went rolling on.

This Big Sam, he played 6,
His story, it just won't stick.
He said: "Sit back on a tack, throw these chumps a bone !"
This Big Sam went rolling on.

This Big Sam, he played 7,
Will he pass by the door to heaven ?
He said: "Sit back on a tack, throw these chumps a bone !"
This Big Sam went rolling on.

This Big Sam, he played 8,
Are you ready for your court date ?
He said: "Sit back on a tack, throw these chumps a bone !"
This Big Sam went rolling on.

This Big Sam, he played 9,
He can whine while doing time.
He said: "Sit back on a tack, throw these chumps a bone !"
This Big Sam went rolling on.

This Big Sam, he played 10,
Just start over, sing again.
He said: "Sit back on a tack, throw these chumps a bone !"
This Big Sam went rolling on.

IF THE GRAY HAT FITS, QUIT WEARING IT !

* * REQUIRED MEMORIZATION FOR ALL LAW SCHOOL STUDENTS * *

Once upon a time, not so long ago, and not so far away, there was a group of dedicated, sincere, hard-working, diligent lawyers who struggled long, long years without pay. They are called the WHITE-HAT-WEARERS. The WHITE-HAT-WEARERS' goal was to expose the evil deeds of some bad, bad guys called the BLACK-HAT-WEARERS. The BLACK-HAT-WEARERS were responsible for years and years of wrongs done to a great crowd of individuals. In the course of time, the relentless efforts of the WHITE-HAT-WEARERS forced the BLACK-HAT-WEARERS to their knees, and the WHITE-HAT-WEARERS ordered the BLACK-HAT-WEARERS to "Pay up, or else..." ! The BLACK-HAT-WEARERS looked up and saw the great throng of unhappy, worthy, waiting, watching individuals, called CLASS-PLAINTIFFS. The BLACK-HAT-WEARERS knew the deal was up and offered to pay huge sums of "undisclosed amounts" called SETTLEMENTS, but to only a very few of the great throng of unhappy, worthy, waiting, watching individuals, called CLASS-PLAINTIFFS. And the WHITE-HAT-WEARERS also got their just deserves, call CONTINGENCY-FEES. (You do the math.)

But that's where the winding, bumpy road takes an ugly, downward turn. There still remained a great throng of unhappy, worthy, waiting, watching individuals, called CLASS-PLAINTIFFS who also had been harmed by the BLACK-HAT-WEARERS, and were yet uncompensated by SETTLEMENTS. The problem was that the WHITE-HAT-WEARERS now were wealthy enough to buy a new set of hats in varying shades of GRAY. Plus, the former WHITE-HAT-WEARERS' stomachs and wallets were over stuffed, causing them to slow down to a snail's pace. A few of the former WHITE-HAT-WEARERS stopped moving at all. They became permanent charcoal GRAY-HAT-WEARERS, and started to let their answering services take messages from the great throng of unhappy, worthy, waiting, watching individuals, called CLASS-PLAINTIFFS. Some of the GRAY-HAT-WEARERS began to view the great throng of unhappy, worthy, waiting, watching individuals, called CLASS-PLAINTIFFS, as expendable, unneeded, irritants, and nuisances. The remaining GRAY-HAT-WEARERS adopted the role of presenting chump-change, take-it-or-leave-it unsettling SETTLEMENT offers doled out from the BLACK-HAT-WEARERS. Those GRAY-HAT-WEARERS' frequently heard mantra became: "If I were you I'd take this offer and run with it. It doesn't get better than this." (Talk about verse #2 of the song that never ends...Repeat it 3X with a rhythm and you'll get the hang of it.)

Anyway, many of the great throng of unhappy, worthy, waiting, watching individuals, called CLASS-PLAINTIFFS were so frustrated and distraught that they gave up and lost all faith in the legal system as a means to address grievances and wrongs. You see, the great throng of unhappy, worthy, waiting, watching individuals, called CLASS-PLAINTIFFS never trusted BLACK-HAT-WEARERS to start with, but they had let down their guard and had started to grow fond of WHITE-HAT-WEARERS. (Boo-Hoo.) But now the great throng of unhappy, worthy, waiting, watching individuals, called CLASS-PLAINTIFFS told their friends, family, and anyone else who would listen that no WHITE-HAT-WEARERS were to be trusted either because when WHITE-HAT-WEARERS get fat wallets and full stomachs, they start to wear all shades of GRAY-HATS. And worse than that, when some GRAY-HAT-WEARERS get their gold watches, they will not even give the great throng of unhappy, worthy, waiting, watching individuals, called CLASS-PLAINTIFFS, the time of day !!!

Shame on them.

But one individual emerged from the great throng of unhappy, worthy, waiting, watching individuals, called CLASS-PLAINTIFFS and declared: "This must not continue. For the sake of future great throngs of unhappy, worthy, waiting, watching individuals, called CLASS-PLAINTIFFS, this wrong too must be addressed." This individual then offered the following remedy:

Until the WHITE-HAT-WEARERS see to it that all of the cooperating members of the great throng of unhappy, worthy, waiting, watching individuals, called CLASS-PLAINTIFFS are compensated by the BLACK-HAT-WEARERS, the courts will hold the CONTINGENCY FEES of the WHITE-HAT-WEARERS. The courts will allow only the interim reimbursement of reasonable and well-documented litigation related expenses.

And in the course of time, this rule, or code, or canon was enacted and practiced all throughout the land. Neither the WHITE-HAT-WEARERS, or the BLACK-HAT-WEARERS, or the GRAY-HAT-WEARERS were very pleased. But the great throng of worthy, waiting, watching individuals, called CLASS-PLAINTIFFS was exuberant!!! They insisted on calling this new rule, or code, or canon "The Bailey Principle". Really, they insisted. And so the great throng of worthy, waiting, watching individuals, called CLASS-PLAINTIFFS lived happily ever after, or something like that.

IBM'S PALMISANO DANCE

SAM PUTS HIS RIGHT HAND IN,

SAM PULLS HIS LEFT HAND OUT;

SAM EXERCISES OPTIONS,

AND SAM SHAKES THEM ALL ABOUT.

SAM DOES THE SELL-SELL POKEY,

SAM THEN TURNS MULTI-MILLION$$$ 'ROUND.

AND THAT'S WHAT BIG SAM'S ABOUT !

SELL-SELL POKEY !

O Sammy Mean, Mean, Mean

O Sammy mean, mean, mean
All dressed in Green$, Green$, Green$,
While stock proceeds, misdeeds,
Bust pocket seams, seams, seams.

Let's ask Big Blue Execs
'Bout their stock trades, trades, trades,
When they joined hands, hands, hands,
Big Blue to raid, raid, raid.

The stock went high, high, high,
Near to the sky, sky, sky;
SMART PLANETeerers no tears,
Wave us good bye, bye, bye.

Hello, Bernie Madoff,
Move over more, more, more;
We'll trade war tales and lore,
'Til our lips are sore, sore, sore.

"IBM'S BIG SAM PRANCES TO THE BANK WITH HIS UNCLE SAMS"

1-2-3

I have to slap my knee !

4-5-6

Boy, I pulled some trick !

7-8-9

Stockholders left behind !

So when I get to 10,

You bet, I will start again !!!

10-9-8

It was a piece of cake !

7-6-5

I am so slick, I'm jive !

4-3-2

I don't care 'bout you !

I am number 1, Watch me -

'Cause I am not done !!!

The Big Blue Son

Big Sam, bold moves
Big dreams, wild run.
He makes his name
On the Blue Sun.

History books
May say: "Da Mon" –
He's some genius !
This Big Blue Son !

The Real Big One
Sits up on high,
Looking below –
Big Sam, "Bye-Bye!"

Portrait Of Big Sam

Sticky fingers ?

Twinkle toes ?

When in doubt,

Wiggle nose !

All now is mine,

Let joy bells ring.

I'm royalty –

Me is The King !

Big Sam Acrostic

S is for savvy, a slick chap, indeed.

A is for agile, lift high, bend those knees !

M is for manage, manipulate, move.

U is to utilize any means "I won't lose !"

E – that was easy, for a SMART man like me.

L – I'll live to get rich, retire, and go free !

Big Sam's No Jolly Good Fellow

Big Sam's no jolly good fellow, [3X]
And everyone now can agree.
And everyone now can agree,
He fleeced the Big Blue, you, and me.
Big Sam's no jolly good fellow, [3X]
And everyone now can agree.

Big Sam's no jolly good fellow, [3X]
His Big Blue stock sales will decry !
And nobody can deny,
With brazen, he did defy.
Big Sam's no jolly good fellow, [3X]
And nobody can deny.

Big Blue's SMARTest

Flip over my stocks.

Churn options – pounce, pounce.

Max out share profits.

Optimize – bounce, bounce.

We are the SMARTest,

Or, so we once thought.

Our scheme is on Blast !

Help, yikes, we've been caught !!!

3 IBMketeers

Big Sam, SMART Mark, Cheap Bob,

Looked high into the sky.

They set their sights above –

Told the Dow Jones – "Bye-Bye" !

They outSMARTed the rest,

Because they are The Best !

Insiders rules they test –

Their bank accounts are blest !

A Crash Course

You tell a Big Fib,

And I'll swear it's so.

Just stick to your line,

Not two, three words more !

When Congress questions

You behind closed door,

Don't vary your speech.

If pressed, stomp the floor !

Phantom Stocks

Phantom stocks are spooking.

Derivative, confusing.

Indirects, misleading.

All in all, deceiving.

Plan D – Prison dungeon.

Plan C – Come clean, Execs.

Plan B – Bunk mate, Madoff.

Plan A – Tell all, confess !

Everybody's Got A Cover Story

Tuition payments.
A second home.
Trip round the world –
Let my heart roam.

Wedded bliss –
My trophy bride.
A yacht, chalet,
A Rolls Royce ride.

I could go on,
With more baloney.
But alimony's
My testimony !

IBM – The Titanic

Too Big to sail ?

Too Big to fail ?

Big Execs, Big sales,

Big Houses – Big jails !

Dark CLOUDs ? Blue genes ?

Scofflaws – The Scene ?

Big Execs, Big jails.

WHASSUPS ? Tell ! Tell !

Just Call Me Bunk Mate !

Move over, Madoff,
I need lots more space.
I stretch, bend, and yawn,
All over the place !

We've plenty to share,
Our tales of misdeeds -
Let me begin mine,
So others may heed.

Insiders, beware –
Temptations and vice.
Too much is at risk:
Fed time is not nice !

If You're Unhappy, And You Know It

If you're unhappy and you know it, say Boo-Hoo, Boo-Hoo. [2X]
If you're unhappy and you know it,
Then your Big Blue face will show it.
If you're unhappy and you know it, say Boo-Hoo, Boo-Hoo.

If you're on your way to jail, don't clap your hands, your hands. [2X]
If you're on your way to jail,
'Cause your alibi won't sail.
If you're on your way to jail, don't clap your hands, your hands.

As you do your years, repent and bow your head, your head. [2X]
As you do your years for crimes,
Seek forgiveness, do not whine.
As you do your years, repent and bow your head, your head.

Standing In the Need of Prayer

Refrain

It's me, it's me, it's me, Big Sam,
Standing in the need of prayer. [Repeat both lines.]

Verse 1

And my lawyers, and my brokers, plus it's me, Big Sam,
Standing in the need of prayer. [Repeat both lines.]

Refrain

Verse 2

It's my family, and my colleagues, and it's me, Big Sam,
Standing in the need of prayer. [Repeat both lines.]

Refrain [2X]

Don't Run, Don't Hide !

What is your Bernie Madoff side ?
What is that something you still hide ?
Do you sneak in a drink or puff ?
Oh, 'fess up now, and do not bluff !

"Our secret sins will find us out,"
The Good Book says, there is no doubt !
In time, that which you do conceal,
Will jump up front, your past to spill.

While there's yet time for you to change,
Refocus, regroup, rearrange !
The clock ticks fast, it's not your friend.
But God will help you 'til the end.

POSTLUDE

Much of this poetry might be considered comical or entertaining. The main purpose is not to ridicule individuals but to grab them by their shoulders and challenge them and the readers to ponder their ways.

He who finishes with the most toys might be the loser !

"For what shall it profit a man, if he shall gain the whole world, and lose his own soul ?
Or what shall a man give in exchange for his soul ?"

Mark 8:36,37

Read that verse out loud at least 3X. Let it sink in.

The news is full of highly placed men and women who fell from grace because of personal and business indiscretions. Why add your name to that lengthy list ?

Other endeavors of Madame P. J. Bailey include:

http://ibmTheWidowMaker.com
http://Twitter.com/MadamePJBailey (IBM Widow)

http://PrayToGodForOBAMA.com
http://Twitter.com/PrayersForOBAMA

http://GODsTWEET.com
http://Twitter.com/GODsTWEET

TEA

PARTY

TANTRUMS

VOLUME 1

BY MADAME P. J. BAILEY

FREE DOWNLOAD ON -

PrayToGodForOBAMA.com

DEDICATION:

TO ALL THE POOR OR VOICELESS.

GOAL:

Hold up a mirror to Tea Party members, and those of like spirit, in the hope that they will glimpse their stony hearts, and seek softer ones of flesh !

(Ezekiel 11:19; 36:26)

◇ ◇ ◇ ◇ ◇ ◇

"I said unto the fools, Deal not foolishly: and to the wicked, Lift not up the horn: Lift not up your horn on high: speak not with a stiff neck. For promotion cometh neither from the east, nor from the west, nor from the south. But God is the judge: he putteth down one, and setteth up another."

PSALM 75: 4-7

INDEX TO <u>TEA PARTY TANTRUMS</u>

INTRODUCTION TO VOLUME 1 –

TEA PARTY TANTRUMS

I generally do not watch TV. But in late July and early August 2011, I visited my 94 year old aunt. TV is her regular companion and I joined in her interest. I might add that my aunt is a retired school teacher who relies in part on Social Security and Medicare protection.

We watched and discussed the Congressional debates concerning the default and deficit. As I listened to speeches and news shows, I wrote down phrases and snippets of discourse. I arranged these tidbits into short poems. I decided to release Volume 1 as a FREE download, while I work on completing Volumes 2 and 3.

Please read, comment, and share.

The E-mail link appears on - PrayToGodForOBAMA.com

Please visit - TWITTER - PrayersForOBAMA

Verbal Tantrums Of Bullies and Cry Babies
By Madame P. J. Bailey

I want bottle !
I need my nap !
Don't touch my toys !
I bite ! I snap !

No place in House
To throw tantrums.
Tea Patriots
Beat loud on drums.

Let Congress know
To rein them in.
They are not cute.
We do not grin.

I Won't Be My Brother's Keeper !
By Madame P. J. Bailey

A new selfishness is rising
From one sea to shining sea.
I won't be my brother's keeper -
I don't care except for me.

He can sleep on cold park benches,
'Cause he's a lazy, shiftless one.
Let him get a job, and quickly.
"Pull up by boot straps, then run."

I give no thought to how your children
Fare at school, at home, beyond.
What you eat, or if you eat,
Bores me so I start to yawn.

Just don't ask for health assistance -
Medicaid goes to those bums,
'Cept my parents' nursing home care:
I worked the rules, I saved <u>BIG</u> sums !!!

When the Bible says to love folk,
I re-write it just a bit.
I decide who I will help out –
Press me more, I'll have a fit !!!

What's In Your DNA ?
By Madame P. J. Bailey

What's in your DNA ?
What's in your cold heart ?
Slash Medicare and schools –
Your brain is not smart !

Oil execs hold slush funds
While elderly starve.
What kind of DNA ?
What kind of cold heart ?

The voters will dissect
Your DNA strand,
Expose your corruption.
You'll be sorry you ran !

Credit Where Fault Is Due
By Madame P. J. Bailey

Throwing little weight around,
Throwing tantrums, fits.
Tea party's 5 seconds of fame,
Like a movie bit.

But the fallout for the world –
Rates of interest rise.
'Caused by the default impasse –
Disaster streaks the skies !

Tour Guide To The Dark Side
By Madame P. J. Bailey

Let's visit Greed Row,
Where bankers hang out.
Then onto Mean Street,
Those Patriots lurk 'bout.

If you like the rough life,
When you hear a Big Mouth,
Just turn left on Selfish –
Tea Boulevard South.

My Kind of Constituents
By Madame P. J. Bailey

I smile and cheese for photo opts.
But if you're poor, no pity.
I like bankers, corp execs:
Rich folk get me quite giddy !

I Got Mine
By Madame P. J. Bailey

I got mine,
If you get yours
Without my help
To open doors,

Good luck, you Chumps,
Poor blokes, fat chance !
Won't match my wealth –
I dine, I dance !

Talking 'Bout "Patriots" True Color
By Madame P. J. Bailey

Your true color is green,
And you are real mean !
You create quite a scene,
When 'ere you let off steam.

You huff, puff and pout,
Pound fists, stomp about.
Tea Party's so stout -
Great Society's in doubt.

In Your Best Interest
By Madame P. J. Bailey

Your best interest's at heart,
Ha-Ha, Hee-Hee !
You need never fear fraud,
Oh no ? Ho-Ho !

A three-fifth vote is best,
Ha-Ha, Hee-Hee !
Broad powers you test,
Oh yes, Ho-Ho !

But people don't trust,
Oh no, Oh no !
Your protests go bust,
Oh yes, Oh yes !

Instincts: Red Alert –
Rough ride in the dirt,
2012 you'll go !
Oh no, Oh no !

Disparities
By Madame P. J. Bailey

You measure wealth by stock shares,
I gaze on my pantry shelf.
If I have some food for next week,
I'm elated: I'm bereft.

If we speak about our incomes,
"Per annum" may be your term.
I explain my wage in hours,
And for pennies more, I yearn.

If we look 'round 'bout our dwellings,
Analyze then our health opts –
I barely afford my co-pays,
You pick specialists: The Top !

Let's not talk of school choice –
My kid's going in the 'hood,
'Cause the alternative, the teaser
Is a joke, I understood.

But a time 'fore long is coming,
When we'll stand before THE JUDGE -
Not the one in your back pocket:
You will feel His Mighty Nudge !

From Dream To Nightmare
By Madame P. J. Bailey

I had a sweet dream
That turned to nightmare.
Tea Patriots' zeal –
Tea Party's unfair.

'Cause they do not feel
The pain of the poor.
The little man's pleas
Don't get through their door !

It took years to build up
Great Society's Trust,
But a few months with them
They'll dismantle, corrupt.

YourPappy Said
By Madame P. J. Bailey

Your Pappy said:
Don't take no stuff;
Don't give one inch –
Stand firm, be gruff !

No compromise,
No give or take.
My way, or else:
Poor Rep you'll make !

'Cause Congressmen
Must listen, learn;
Respect their peers.
Be flex, not stern.

Hit The Reset Button
(Not The Panic Button)
By Madame P. J. Bailey

Reset debate to jobs,
'Cause USA's debt ceiling
Doesn't matter very much
As we sit in our small kitchen.

What can we do for jobs ?
How shall we pay our bill ?
Keep creditors assured ?
We'll pray and then "Be still !"

Crisis on Main Street
By Madame P. J. Bailey

A crisis is on Main Street,
At kitchen tables here.
No TV cameras gathered,
To record our dreads, our fears.

The microphones are silent,
As savings dwindle out;
Retirement plans are voided
Prescriptions, food's in doubt.

There's no trouble down in your way,
On the cul-de-sac, your yard.
But the tears that flow in my house
Will soon smear, ruin your regard.

I Want To Make It Here !
By Madame P. J. Bailey

Make it here in the USA
So I can make it here.
I need a job with good wages
To support family dear.

Shift earnings, level playing field –
Bring jobs from other shore.
Build in America the Great:
Not working makes us sore !

We'll remember when we go vote,
We won't forget the pain.
We know the names who played the games –
Then see who goes insane !

Meet Me On The Bridge
By Madame P. J. Bailey

Please come right cross this bridge.
Meet me at the mid point.
Let's look for common cares,
Leave aside the disjoint.

There's so much that's at stake;
Time's ticking, crises loom.
Let's be more proactive –
Earth is but one small room.

My survival, your own -
Entwined more than you know.
Sooner, not later times
You will reap that which you sow !

Mayflowers' Great-Grands
By Madame P. J. Bailey

Your folks sailed to these shores
Abroad the old Mayflower.
They kissed US's rich soil,
Prospered, gained wealth and power.

So you're an Immigrant,
Just like these recent fellows.
Your mirror will reflect
You should be much more mellow !

Have empathy, not scorn,
For the newest arrivals.
Their successes or failures,
Seal your fates and survival !!!

Mud Pies
By Madame P. J. Bailey

Don't throw mud pies at me
'Cause I'm on Medicare.
I worked long years earning this "gift" –
Don't snatch it unaware

That I've no deep cushion,
To prop me should I fall.
You're not my Representative,
If you don't care at all !

Dumping Baby Out With Bath
By Madame P. J. Bailey

You don't just get it Tea Party –
Your hands are tied to mine !
When you interrupt my air flight,
Your daughter's in a bind

When she travels to her college
At the same time, my son.
With slashes to grants, student aid –
Her class may get undone !

A Different Set of Rules
By Madame P. J. Bailey

US Presidents all look alike –
Except for one.

They got benefit of doubt –
Except for one.

None called a "liar" during a House address –
Except for one.

Few walked with such quiet dignity while vilified –
Except for one !

www.ingramcontent.com/pod-product-compliance
Lightning Source LLC
Chambersburg PA
CBHW052052190326
41519CB00002BA/194